SMOKEJUMPERS

by Jim Gigliotti

Published by The Child's World®
800-599-READ • www.childsworld.com

Copyright © 2023 by The Child's World®
All rights reserved. No part of this book may be reproduced or utilized in any form or by any means without written permission from the publisher.

Photography Credits
Cover: Dreamstime.com.
Interior: AP Photo: Elaine Thompson 10; The Bulletin/Pete Erickson 11; Gordon Robinson/Yakima Herald-Republic 15; Michael Gallagher/Missoulian 21. Courtesy Santa Barbara County Fire Department/Mike Eliason: 6, 16, 18, 19, 26, 27, 28. Shutterstock: VanderWolf Images 7; S.J. Robinson 17; Alex Traveler 22; Moises Br. 29. US Forest Service: 7 (2), 8. USDA: 5, 9, 12, 13, 14, 20, 23, 24 (2), 25.

ISBN Information
9781503858183 (Reinforced Library Binding)
9781503860780 (Portable Document Format)
9781503862142 (Online Multi-user eBook)
9781503863507 (Electronic Publication)

LCCN 2021952456

Printed in the United States of America

SMOKEJUMPERS

TABLE OF CONTENTS

CHAPTER 1
One-of-a-Kind Job . . . 4

CHAPTER 2
Tools of the Trade . . . 12

CHAPTER 3
Fire Call! . . . 20

GLOSSARY . . . 30
THINK ABOUT IT . . . 31
FIND OUT MORE . . . 31
INDEX . . . 32
ABOUT THE AUTHOR . . . 32

CHAPTER 1

ONE-OF-A-KIND JOB

Rick Rataj stands in the open doorway of an airplane. He is flying high above a forest where a fire is raging. Most people would be worried, but Rick is ready to go to work.

Rick is a smokejumper—a special kind of firefighter who uses a **parachute** to jump into the forest to fight fires. Without smokejumpers, it might take many hours — even days — to reach a **remote** fire. The smokejumpers' speed can mean saving hundreds of **acres** of forest. Getting these highly-trained people to the fire quickly also saves property, animals, and sometimes even people.

Smokejumpers float down into danger. These firefighters will land and head to the fire behind.

After landing, smokejumpers gather their gear before fighting the fire.

To be a smokejumper, you need to have basic firefighting skills as well as experience fighting wildfires. You also need to be an expert parachutist and be in peak physical and mental condition. The work is difficult and long. Smokejumpers face demanding workdays that can last up to 16 hours.

In this daring job, you need a sense of adventure and excitement, too.

"I learned the excitement of jumping out of planes in the military," Rick says. "I knew it was fun to jump out of an airplane, so I was fired up to go into smokejumping."

SMOKEJUMPER HISTORY

World War I (1914-1918) showed how airplanes could be used in many ways. In 1934, the U.S. Forest Service started exploring ways to use airplanes to help fight forest fires. During a 1940 fire in Idaho's Nez Perce National Forest, smokejumpers Rufus Robinson and Earl Cooley became the first to jump into a fire zone to work. Since then, thousands of smokejumpers have worked around the world.

Since 1981, women have ever been part of America's smokejumpers.

Smokejumpers are a select group of men and women. There are only about 400 in the United States—and only about 20 new jumpers are hired each year.

Because they are few in number, and because it is such a difficult and dangerous job, smokejumpers are a **close-knit** group. When they are not in the forest fighting fires, they are back at the base station helping each other out.

Checking over parachutes is a big part of getting ready to go to work.

Everyone has different responsibilities. Some jumpers repair parachutes, while others pack boxes of food. The smokejumpers will be away from home for days at a time. They have to carry what they need to eat and drink. Other smoke jumpers repair chainsaws and check other tools.

All smokejumpers have to pass a physical test before they are hired. They have to pass it again every spring. Among the tests: run a mile and a half (2 km) in less than 11 minutes.

Candidates have to do a series of 7 pull-ups, 25 push-ups, and 45 sit-ups. They must also jog a three-mile (5 km) course in less than 45 minutes—all while carrying a 45-pound (20 kg) pack. It's even harder than it sounds!

Smokejumpers need to stay in excellent physical shape. Each day after **roll call**, jumpers work out for 90 minutes. They can run, swim, lift weights, or bike. Smokejumpers' hard work in the gym pays off with safe work in the field.

These firefighters are training for the test to be smokejumpers.

Parachute training starts closer to the ground off towers, with jumpers attached to wires.

CHAPTER 2

TOOLS OF THE TRADE

The parachute is the main piece of equipment that separates a smokejumper from other firefighters.

Before every jump, the smokejumpers inspect their parachutes for rips or tears. Then the parachutes are refolded and repacked. An inspector signs off on them, and they are ready for the next jump. All jumpers carry a main parachute on their back and a smaller, backup parachute in the front. Good preparation makes for safe jumping.

After supervisors check their gear (left), smokejumpers head to the airplane. They wear parachutes and carry packs of gear.

Smokejumpers wear canvas jumpsuits. The pants have pockets for items such as a 150-foot (46-m) "letdown rope," used when a jumper gets stuck in a tree.

The helmet has wire **mesh** over the face to keep the jumper from getting scraped by branches or rocks. A jumper's thick gloves offer extra protection, too.

One item every jumper carries (but hopes never to need) is a fire shelter. It's a small, shiny, silver tent. When surrounded by fire, the jumper can crawl into this tent. The silver material protects the jumper from the intense heat.

The masks protect the jumpers if they land in trees.

A firefighter demonstrates how they climb into protective fire shelters.

Smokejumpers need more than they can carry with them, however. After dropping the jumpers, the airplane returns and drops boxes attached to big parachutes. The boxes, which are full of gear, drift down to the smokejumpers.

These are the boxes the jumpers packed during their time at the base. Some of the boxes contain canned food, snacks, and water to give the jumpers energy during the hours—or days—ahead.

Other boxes have the heavy-duty firefighting equipment the jumpers need to do their job. They'll use shovels, chainsaws, picks, axes, and a special tool for fighting forest fires called a **Pulaski**.

Parachute jumps take firefighters near the fire, but they also might have to hike in.

Using a Pulaski, this smokejumper is breaking up a flaming tree stump.

The Pulaski is a two-in-one tool for both chopping and making trenches. It is one of the smokejumper's most useful tools. The Pulaski's head has an axe on one side and a hoe on the other, which helps when digging trenches. The tool is named for Edward Pulaski, a ranger who invented it in the early 1900s.

Chainsaws and shovels help clear away brush and trees. Another one-of-a-kind tool is a **drip torch**, which is used to start **backfires**.

Why start a fire? By creating this kind of small, controlled fire, the smokejumper can help put out the main fire. That's because fire usually can't burn over an area that has already been burned.

A backfire lit by a drip torch can stop a larger fire from spreading.

CHAPTER 3

FIRE CALL!

A loud horn sounds at the base station. Someone has spotted a fire in the forest! It's time for the smokejumpers to move into action.

All the jumpers head to their lockers and put on their gear as quickly as possible. They grab their parachutes and a personal-gear bag that includes their fire shelter, snacks, and maybe some extra socks.

Packed parachutes are ready when the smokejumpers are called.

Before boarding the plane that will take them to the **drop spot**, each jumper works with a "buddy" to check each other's equipment one more time. Then they're good to go!

Safety first: The jumpers all check each other's gear one more time.

21

A small fire, perhaps one tree that has been struck by lightning, might need only two or three jumpers. But a larger fire, maybe a 10-acre (4 ha) blaze, might take eight to 10 jumpers. Once the jumpers are aboard the plane, they head to a clear jump spot. Jumpers are only dropped into safe areas, away from trees that might tangle the parachutes.

"We always jump to a clear spot, so we can be sure we're safe," Rick says. "You can almost always find a clear area or an opening in the **forest canopy**.

"We look for a meadow, a log deck, a road . . . anything big enough for us to jump safely in there."

Spotters note where the flames are and look for a safe spot nearby.

Most smokejumpers now use rectangular parachutes that can be steered more easily than rounder ones.

A crew member drops several streamers of colored paper out of the plane to see which way the wind is blowing. Then, when the pilot gives the all-clear signal, the jumpers leap out the door!

The jumpers drift down toward the drop zone, landing softly (they hope!). Then they gather their parachutes. They agree on a "safety zone," a nearby area where they'll meet in case of emergency.

Time to jump! The parachute begins coming out as soon as the jumper leaves the plane.

The spotter keeps track of the jumpers as they reach land.

They examine the area and check their **compasses**. They get final instructions from their crew leader.

"Then it's time for the not-so-fancy part of the job," Rick says. For the brave smokejumpers, it's time to grab a chainsaw and a Pulaski and get to work!

READ THE WIND

Streamers dropped by the spotter—and flags set up by earlier jumpers—help smokejumpers see which way and how fast the wind is blowing. This helps them land safely.

Creating a fire line is hard, dirty work. Hoses can sometimes be stretched in to help.

After hiking to the fire, the jumpers' first order of business is creating a fire line. That's a cleared strip around the fire, like a trail, to rob the fire of the fuel that it needs to burn. Jumpers use their chainsaws, shovels, and other equipment to clear away brush or trees—anything that the fire can use as fuel.

The jumpers dig down to the soil, which does not burn. For small fires, the fire line might be only a couple of feet wide. For big fires, it might be several yards across.

As they reach the flames, firefighters try to create a fire line to stop the flames' advance.

After the blaze is contained with a fire line, the smokejumpers begin "mop-up" work to put the fire out completely. To do this, they'll mix and stir the dirt with water to cool the ashes down.

Once the fire is totally out, it's time for the jumpers to get on their hands and knees. They feel the fire area to make sure there's no heat left on the ground.

Mopping up is the last step. The firefighters make sure all the "hot spots" are put out.

The fire is out! The smokejumpers' job is done. Their hard work and training have paid off. Now it's time to pack up and head back to the base—and get ready for the next fire call.

DANGER INCREASES

Scientists say that **climate change** is increasing the danger of wildfires every year. The air temperature is increasing and less rain is falling, leading to dry, dangerous forest conditions. More and more people are also building homes in areas that might catch fire. Smokejumpers and other firefighters will likely have a lot of dangerous work to do.

GLOSSARY

acres (AKE-ers) a unit of measure for large areas of land (1 acre = 43,560 square feet or 4,047 square meters)

backfires (BAK-fyres) fires started on purpose to burn away fuel so a forest fire can't advance

climate change (KLY-mut CHAYNJ) a shift in Earth's weather patterns and temperatures

close-knit (KLOSE-NIT) having a very tight relationship with one another

compasses (KUM-puss-es) devices used to tell direction, with a magnetic needle that always points north

drip torch (DRIP TORCH) a tool that drips fuel and flame to start backfires and other carefully controlled outdoor fires

drop spot (DROP SPOT) the safe area where the smokejumpers are supposed to land

forest canopy (FORE-est KAN-uh-pee) the high covering formed by the meeting of treetops above a forest

mesh (MESH) a net made of woven wires or threads with spaces in between

parachute (PARE-uh-shoot) a piece of light, strong cloth that lets a person or an object float safely to the ground from an airplane

Pulaski (puh-LASS-kee) a fire-fighting tool with an axe and a hoe

remote (ree-MOAT) far away from people or buildings

roll call (ROLL CALL) a way of taking attendance

THINK ABOUT IT

Do you want to be a smokejumper? Why or why not?

Why do you think smokejumpers spend so much time checking their gear? Explain your answer.

How might homeowners in forested areas be able to help smokejumpers?

FIND OUT MORE

IN THE LIBRARY

Jones, Emma. *Smokejumpers*. New York, NY: PowerKids Press, 2016.

Potenza, Alessandra. *All About Wildfires*. New York, NY: Children's Press/Scholastic, 2021.

Seigel, Rachel. *California and Other Western Wildfires*. New York, NY: Crabtree, 2019.

ON THE WEB

Visit our website for links about smokejumpers and wildfires:
childsworld.com/links

*Note to Parents, Teachers, and Librarians:
We routinely verify our Web links to make sure they are safe and active sites. So encourage your readers to check them out!*

INDEX

airplanes, 4, 7, 16, 21, 22
backfires, 19
Cooley, Earl, 7
drip torch, 19
drop spot, 22, 24
fire call, 9, 29
fire line, 26, 27, 28
fire shelter, 15
food, 9, 17
forest fires, 4-6, 8, 22, 26-29
jumpsuits, 14
letdown rope, 14
Nez Perce National Forest, 7
parachutes, 4, 6, 9, 12, 16, 20, 21, 24
pilot, 24
Pulaski, 17, 18, 25
Pulaski, Edward, 18
Rataj, Rick, 4, 7, 22, 25
Robinson, Rufus, 7
smokejumpers
    creating fire line, 26
    gear, 13, 14, 17, 25, 26
    mopping up, 28
    physical training, 10, 29
    setting backfires, 19
    women, 8
tools, firefighting, 9, 14, 17-19, 25, 26
wildfire, 29

ABOUT THE AUTHOR

JIM GIGLIOTTI has written dozens of nonfiction books for young readers. His specialty is sports and biographies, and he has written several of the well-known "Who Was…?" books. He lives in Oregon.